Survival Guide for an Impossible World

Free
Happiness Business
Singles
Workplace
Reasons for Good News
Diets
Waiting

Paul T. Owens

Copyright © 2011 by Paul T. Owens. All rights reserved.

Published by Myron Publishers. No part of this publication may be reproduced, transmitted, transcribed, stored in a retrieval system, or translated into any language, in any form by any means without the written permission of the publisher; exceptions are made for brief excerpts used in published reviews.

Published by
Myron Publishers
4625 Saltillo St.
Woodland Hills, CA 91364
www.myronpublishers.com
www.paultowens.com

ISBN:978-0-9824675-2-7
Printed in the USA

This book is available for purchase in bulk by organizations and institutions at special discounts. Please direct your inquiries to sales@MyronPublishers.com

Editing by Lee Fields and Jo Ellen Krumm
Cover, Interior Design, Typesetting by Lyn Adelstein

What People are Saying About

Survival Guide for an Impossible World

"Well written, too shocking, too realistic."
　　　　—Foster Quarters

"Conservatives and liberals can finally agree on something . . . This book."
　　　　—Political Context Forum

"This book will make you live better. Better than who is all you have to decide."
　　　　—George G. George

"Finally, a book I should have written myself."
　　　　—Jeremy L.

"Another book you should not read while driving, as it will put you to sleep."
　　　　—Melvin Mavan, Triple Digits Driving College

"A real piece of work. I don't know if it works for you, but it worked for me; how well it works for me, I am still trying to find out, but read it already."
　　　　—Susan S.

"Congratulations. You found it. You might never find the right girl or guy, but this is the right book."
　　　　—Gertrude Zoftick

"I survived. Now what?"
　　　　—I. C. Plotz.

The Author and the Book

Paul T. Owens expands his writing talent to humor with this book, *Survival Guide for an Impossible World*. His credits include features for the New York Times, the Los Angeles Times, serving as Senior Staff Writer with the Los Angeles Olympic Organizing Committee for Peter V. Ueberroth, coaching staff writer for the Dallas Cowboys with Tom Landry, biographer of NFL coaches and officials, along with a collection of books with several creative essays. Mr. Owens attended the University of Southern California and Columbia University.

Survival Guide for an Impossible World is a satirical quest to identify and explain how to endure within an impossible world. From being single, laughter-only diets, how not to wait for anything, and words you must learn to be successful in the workplace, Owens makes living easier for anyone.

How free do you have to be? The risks of being in the happiness business, reasons for good news, things you must know, and percentages of life you must ponder, are also subjects which make this guide a pleasure.

Other Books by Paul T. Owens:
- *Leaners Out of the Wind*, with artist Claudia J. Sobel
- *Don't Hit Him, He's Dead*, with John McDonough, foreword Deacon Jones
- *The Kicking Game*, with Ben Agajanian, foreword Tom Landry
- *Who's Kicking Now*
- *Sports Joys and Gifts of Play*
- *Sports Firsts: Winning Stories*
- *Black Language: American Ethnic Speech*, with Professor Malachi Andrews

Table of Contents

How Free Do You Want to Be?.. 7

Risks of Being in the Happiness Business....................... 11

Reasons for Good News 15

What You Need to Be Good At..................................... 19

Percentages to Ponder... 23

Words At Work 25

How to Survive . . .
    While Waiting for Anything or Anybody.................. 65

Laugh it Off.. 79

Being Single is a Dangerous Sport................................. 95

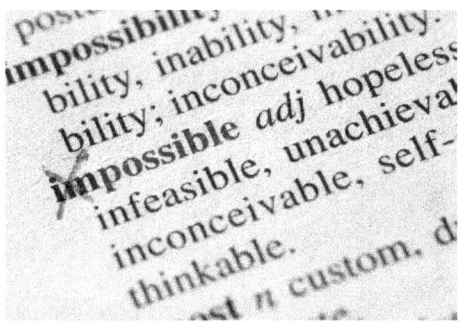

Survival Guide for an Impossible World

How *Free* Do You Want to Be?
How free do you have to be?

You are free to be in your own hurry.
You are free to leave a love without blaming or explaining.
Can you be as free as you want to be?

You are free to believe anything is or was not your fault.

You are free to be taken advantage of.

Free not to overreact to anything.

Free to believe that what just happened did not happen.

Free to thrive on whatever made you happy or makes you unhappy.

Free not to be offended by what others do not do.

Free to think you can continue to like people when they continue to disappoint you.

Free to let someone else retaliate for you.

Free to be silent, imagining how horrific things would be if you said anything.

Free not to care if others do not follow your ideas.

Free to accept compliments and praise as sincere.

Free to realize that those who do not call you back are people you should have not called at all.

Free to create your own grandeur, and listen to your own applause.

Free to celebrate what did not happen as much as you would if it did.

Free to jump to conclusions.

Risks of Being in the Happiness Business

Free to fly off the handle.

Free to push your own luck.

Free to run away from responsibility.

Free to blame someone else.

Free to take credit for what you want to take credit for.

Free to wait forever.

Free to let serendipity decide where you are going, and who you are.

Free to be jealous of yourself.

Free not to lead, or be led.

Free to say what you would rather not say.

ಊ Survival Guide for an Impossible World

Free not to have to explain or change your opinion.

Free to constantly redefine perfection.

Free to be continuously distracted.

Free to give too much information.

Free to make major things minor, and minor things major.

Free to realize that everyone else has the right answers for what you should do and how you should feel.

Free to save your spouse from happiness.

Free, but who is going to pay for it?

Free to announce once and for all that enough is enough already.

Risks of Being in the Happiness Business

If you live long enough, you could possibly get out of the need to be in the happiness business, but the chances of you living that long are not that good. Here are reasons for not wanting to be in the happiness business.

With unhappiness everything is possible.

You must have reasons for not wanting to be in the happiness business.

Happiness is overrated and overly unfulfilling.

Happiness is someone else's fiction.

Why must happiness find you?

Unhappiness comes in every size, fits everyone well.

Luck follows happiness. Got Luck?

Happiness as a profession? What happened?

The job you want is trying to make everyone happy; take it, you will be the most unhappiest of all.

The most fortunate are those who do not choose to be happy.

There is no equity in happiness. Mortgages are still due.

Happiness eliminates responsibility. Why would you not want to have responsibility?

Unhappiness breeds unhappiness. My horse likes your horse.

Wonder why anyone wants to legislate against unhappiness.

What does happiness buy?

Sweets make you fat, not happy.

Risks of Being in the Happiness Business

At least unhappiness won't abandon you.

Imagine everyone happy at the same time. Go ahead.

Money cures all happiness.

You don't have to be happy for winning anything. Think about those who finished second, third, fourth, or not at all.

Show others that you are just as unhappy about their unhappiness as they are.

Unhappiness is blaming everyone else for having the right winning lottery ticket.

Marriage starts as a compromise and happiness ends it.

You don't have to worry when you run out of unhappiness. Someone else will give you another story to bolster your reality.

Remember: If unhappiness is missing, you are not interested.

Reasons for Good News

**If winning prevails, why does there have to be losing?
You accept chaos as an indulgent privilege.**

Good News begins when you realize that this is life, real life, not a dress rehearsal.

To continue good news, you refuse to be around people who choose to feel bad all the time.

You prefer silence, as it does not need a cause, or an opinion.

You can choose your own peace, without your own theatrics.

You can rejoice in not doing everything right.

You must have enough energy at all times to be excited.

When those you did not want to come do not show.

Survival Guide for an Impossible World

The best times were back then. Whatever happens, back then was best.

You are looking for things to do that do not take any effort at all.

You are inspiring yourself to create your own enthusiasm. Even being bored has to be done with enthusiasm.

You find a way to avoid the unavoidable.

You always find a way not to be affected by what someone just did.

You try not to dislike anyone who did not vote as you did.

You try not to listen to anyone's conversation with themselves.

What counts is not how hard you work, but how easy you live.

Success is measured by how well you navigate your television set, how you ABC—Avoid Bad Channels.

Reasons for Good News

You are attempting to master the art of not making choices.

You know that you cannot love someone who does not love you.

It is always easiest to make things more difficult.

Eventually, you do not want to know anything; even the good news can wait.

ಊ Survival Guide for an Impossible World

What You Must Be Good At

**You can't survive without:
Knowing that what goes around does not
always come around.
Not giving those who lied to you once,
a chance to do it again.**

Good at reinventing yourself right in the middle of a sentence.

Good at everything, one thing at a time.

Good at discovering something better in what seems to be getting worse.

Good at having a good time with a bad time.

Good at creating the apology someone else should be giving you.

Good at remembering what you were talking about when you were interrupted.

Good at getting along with those who do not get along with anyone else.

Good at knowing that what goes around does not always come around.

Good at not losing the winning lottery ticket.

Good at being a happy child in the middle of a not so good adult day.

Good at reducing bureaucracy to zero.

Good at giving affirmation and adulation.

Good at believing every coincidence was supposed to have happened.

Good at making someone else's opinion sound like yours.

What You Must Be Good At

Good at making no sound better than yes.

Good at creating drama from absolutely nothing.

Good at realizing how well you have it.

Good at knowing what you don't want to know.

Good at not giving others a chance to lie to you once more.

Good at knowing victory is in the moment, and making each moment a victory.

Good at being your own hero.

Good at realizing that what goes without saying must be said.

You know that there is a reason for everything. It may not be a good reason, you might not know it, but it is there.

Good at remembering the times that the truth was not relevant.

Good at giving someone more than enough chances to be a good person.

Good at not being insulted by anyone else's ignorance.

Good at being your own boss, and bossing yourself around very well.

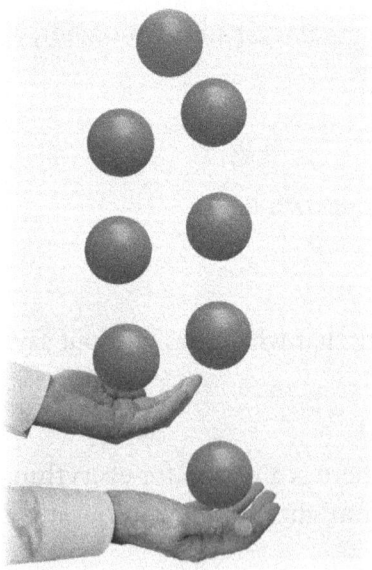

Percentages to Ponder

The percentages must be in your favor:
50% of women are beautiful,
the other 50% do not wear make-up.
50% of all levees fail or have failed,
the other 50% will fail.

80% of the people do not care how you are doing; the other 20% are glad if you are not doing well.

75% of people will exceed an unlimited budget if only given the chance.

90% of coaches of a losing game will believe that their team would have won if the other team's coach was coaching their team.

50% of your work is organizing the other 50% you disorganized.

60% of travelers attempt to find some thing that makes them feel at home; the other 40% are counting the days until they get home.

☙ Survival Guide for an Impossible World

50% of the time you are looking for another job; the other half you are making sure that someone else is doing your current job.

60% of all time is spent avoiding worst case scenarios, while 40% is spent creating them.

50% of the time you are not interesting to anyone else, and the other 50% you are not interesting even to yourself.

50% of advertising budgets are necessary. The dilemma is finding what consists of the 50% that is unnecessary.

60% of children in youth choirs are allowed to sing. The rest are not.

50% of those who riding motor cycles are coming from an accident, the other 50% are going to one.

Of the people you hire to fix something, 25% will tell you why it can't be fixed, the other 75% will break it completely.

90% of people tell those they are leaving a romantic union that, "It's me, not you." The other 10% say, "It's you, not me."

Winning Words at Work

ATLAS---All Time Looker At Suits. One who seeks lawsuits everywhere, holding up the wor[ld]

ATM---Always The Money. It's not the mone[y,] it's the people; it's not the money, it's the worl[d]

ATOM—Admits Their Own Mistakes. The human atomic age is fully realized when ever[y]

ATTITUDE---Always Telling The Truth T[o]

AWWW---Always Want a Way to be Wro[ng]

BAM---Bossing Around Madness. Expre[ss]

Words you must know, meanings you must understand to succeed in your working life.

"This section is for those who want to have fun and be completely productive every day at work."

—Sandy I. Gooder, Vice President,
Global Work Fun Incorporated

A—Anonymous Anonymity. Those who want to remain anonymous to themselves and others, improve their self-doubting, by finding more ways of becoming more and more anonymous.

AA—Adversarial, Antagonistic.

AAA—-Avoiding Adversarial Antagonism.

AAAA—Adults Acting As Adults.

AAAAA—Assistant to An Assistant to An Assistant.

AAAAAA—Accepts Advise Adroitly Assiduously And Accommodatingly—Your job is to make those above you feel more powerful than they are.

ABC—Altercation Beating Chocolate. Beating the urge to satisfy every tense moment with Chocolate craving is an ABC victory.

Abmony—Abmony is the amount of money an employee is paid to be absent from a meeting or event by those who do not want him or her there. Absent costs.

ADAM—Always Dull Aimless Moments The word ADAM is placed next to the person's name on their business card.

Admore—When the advertisement campaign is more clever and convincing than the product is effective, the Admore magic exists.

AKA—Ask Knowing Answers. Don't ask unless you know the answer, and if you can't use it to your advantage.

AND—A New Direction. When the people you are working with tell you that the organization is moving in a new direction, and you will not be included, be glad, why would anyone want to be with those who don't want you moving in their new direction? AND.

ART—Appropriate Reaction Time. Time is an art form. Slowing down to decide how best to react is an art form. Time makes it ART.

ATA—Attacking The Attacker. Those who attack you for what they think you did wrong need to be attacked. Do not give reasons for why you did what you did, just attack the attacker. ATA boy, ATA girl. Most of the time silence is the best ATA, attack verbally later.

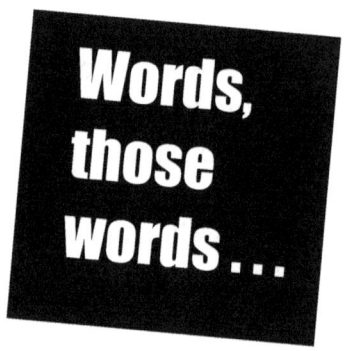

Words, those words...

ATLAS—All Time Litigator At Suits. One who creates lawsuits everywhere, holding up the world for constant legal scrutiny and action. ATLAS, moves through the universe as a devastating human form. The immortal ATLAS remains alive on earth with the excuse of constant litigation as a reason for never having to arrive in heaven.

ATM—Always The Money. It's not the money, it's the people; it's not the money, it's the working conditions; it's not the money, it's the benefits; it's not the money, it's the money. ATM….It's the money—Always The Money.

ATOM—Admits Their Own Mistakes. The human combustible age is fully realized when everyone admits every mistake to those whose reaction they do not want.

ATTITUDE—Always Telling The Inevitable Truth Usually Disconnects Everyone.

AWOOOO—Answer Without Offering One's Own Opinion.

AWWW—Always Want a Way to be Wrong. AWWW, always good to have a reason, rationale for not doing it right, getting it right….AWWW, feels so good to have a way to be wrong and to feel good about the results.

BACKPAY—Boss As Child in Kindergarten; reverts, goes back to. When you decide you are paid to endure the performance of your boss acting as a child in kindergarten, you receive BACKPAY.

BAGS—Bargains At Garage Sale. Ultimate bags time is when all things are bought and sold at garage sales prices.

BAM—Bossing Around Madness. Expressing excessive control and abusive characteristics. BAMers are taught about their madness when any of the people they bossed around become their bosses and become bigger BAMers than they were.

BANG—Being A Nice Girl/Guy. BANG—look what happened because I was too nice . How many BANGers can the work environment accept?

BANK—Better At Not Knowing. What you don't know does better for you than what you do know. BANK on it.

BASIC—But A Successor Is Capable. It's BASIC; if you can't make the meeting, your successor will be capable of attending.

BAW—Both Are Wrong. "BAW. The least wrong, is right."

BEE—Blame Everyone Else. When excuses don't make one less responsible, make a BEE line, and when you cannot blame anyone, pretend it did not happen and then blame someone else for denying that it did not happen.

BEND—Beginning and END. When the beginning and end of an employee's time with the company are close in time, it is said to be a BEND.

BIG—Boss Is Great. Making it BIG is when you are your own boss, and don't like bossing yourself around. You also don't have to ask permission or apologize when something goes wrong.

BIMBA—Boastful Insultive Male Bonding Attitude.

BIMBO—Body Involved Maximally, Brains Overvalued.

BIMP—Bringing In More People. Those who bring more people into a meeting than were originally invited, without permission of anyone are BIMPers.

BIMP—-Boss Is Miserable Person. "It is just that simple; he is a BIMP, such a BIMP I cannot tell you."

BINGO—Best Is Not Good, Obviously. BINGO, we found out what has to be missing in the company, and it is you. We know you are doing your best, however, it is not good enough. And we can only assume that if you improve it still will not be good enough. BINGO, be glad for us that we found this out so that you can be able to look for a place that can use your trying efforts. See AND.

BITO—Body In The Office. LaBITOd is having lost one's job/marriage due to the body in the office.

Blamire—Someone who blames their poor performance on the person/ people who hired them. The poor performer demands that he/she deserves a portion of the salary of the person who hired them as compensation for being placed in an environment where they could not succeed.

BLIB—Better Looking In Box. Someone BLIB spoke glibly while alive, but looked better in the box silent.

BLOC—Boss's Loss of Control. Major source of horror and entertainment is boss in volcanic expressions, totally BLOCING out sanity and decency.

BLUBOOK—Better Left Unsaid. A book filled with things people would like to say; things unsaid that kept everyone and everything together.

BLUNK—Blamed Unknowing. A Blunk occurs when someone is blamed for not doing something they were not told to do. Blunkers vehemently express that they told the blunkees.

BOMB—Boss Of My Boss. When the bossed learns how to boss the boss. When the bossed is elevated above one's boss to be his/her boss, with change in salary and new powers.

BOMB—Bearer Of Misinformation Blatantly—Those responsible for causing unrest because of their incessant repetition of excitable fact and images are BOMBers.

BOND—Brand Of Nothing Doing. A BOND occurs when everyone does nothing at the same time; as in the BONDing philosophy that less is less, not more.

BOO—Bad Options Only. BOO, every option will be the wrong one, the only certainty is that either one will be worse than the rest.

BOOM—Bring One's Own Momentum. Please do not ask your supervisor what is wrong, you need to BOOM into the

Winning Words at Work

office every day. Your purpose is to get paid and create your own morale, momentum, and enthusiasm. Your responsibility is to BOOM every day.

BOOM—Believing One's Own Mystique. Whether initiated by oneself or created by others, BOOMers believe they are what others and themselves mystique them for.

BOP—Blaming Other People. Bopping along is the best way not to be part of the unsuccess all around you.

BOOB—Boss of One's Boss. A BOOB has a fool for his/her employee.

BOOOB—Boss Obvious One Of Blame. BOOOB time all points to the one at the top.

Borepay. The amount of money added to one's salary for the boredom factor of the work.

Boscalvaca—If your boss calls you when you are on vacation for anything, especially something which could have waited until you returned, it is time to look for another job/boss, or be your own boss. If you call your boss for anything while you are on vacation, you don't deserve a vacation and should pay the organization for taking one.

BOSS—#1—Boundless Optimism Sensationally Sensitive.
BOSS—#2—Bullying Oppressive Senseless Seniority.

BOSS—#3—Not Interested In Being Boss, or Bossed. The NIBster is the boss not interested in being a boss.

BOW—Boss Obviously Wrong. What do you do when you cannot tell the boss that he/she is obviously wrong. BOW to their power, quietly, and position yourself so you are not blamed for their mistakes.

BUM—-#1—Best Useless Man.

BUM—-#2—Beat Up Machinery. BUMMING is to beat machinery instead of oneself or others over frequent flights of frustration over what the machinery is not doing for you, and how you cannot seem to know what to do without it. Buscargo—The act of giving a business card you received from someone to someone else thinking it is your own.

BUTBIAS—Born Under The Best Interactive Astrological Sign. Your date of birth has been changed, it now is the date that you first turned on the computer that began dictating your life.

CCC—-Contempt Created by Criticism.

CASING—Complaining About Someone. CASING is something you have to do to deflect from your own shortfalls. No one has to listen, but one has to CASE.

CATS—Complainers About Toys Syndrome. CATS are those who buy excessively expensive toys for the purpose of complaining about the high cost of the toys and the higher cost of maintaining them.

CEO—Cleverest Evader of Obstacles; Cheerleading Every Occasion.

Chanergy—Chaos Energy. The greatest source of energy is chaos.

Cheerdium—Office is like a sport stadium, applause for all effort and scoring success, cheering even for arrival at work, and every great move. A Cheerdium environment is where loud noise and applause are the vocal themes of the day.

CLOP—Cheering Loss Of Power. Clapping silently.

Compexation—Money given to those remaining to cover emotional loss of an employee who has left, as part of the grieving compensation.

Compouter—Someone who spends half of their time COMPlaining about the work they are supposed to do, and the other half making sure someone else is OUT doing it for them.

Comway—Communications done before, particularly on the way to the meeting, accomplishing the purpose of the meeting so that when people meet all they can do is plan other meetings, where everything to be accomplished is done on the way again.

CONSULT—Can Only Navigate Someone else, due to their own Ultimate Lack Of Talent. Those who can't do become consultants so they can agree with those who hire them to agree with their ideas.

Comamittee—The death or elimination of committees and/or meetings.

Conploy—A CONvergence of all ideas from those who are interviewed for emPLOYment. The ideas are utilized to improve the organization, but no one is hired for the position which has now been eliminated.

COO—Chief Official Offender. The person who makes the most offensive comments and moves is the COO.

COP—Criticism Only Praise. Those who defend criticism as the only way to praise are COPing out.

COPES—Change Of Perspective Every Second.

CORE—Conceding Of Responsibility. CORE employees feel they are paid to make sure someone else takes responsibility for their own mistakes.

CROP—Constant Rearranging Of Paper. CROPing is the making and remaking of an art collage from the shapes and sizes of the paper on one's desk.

CUTS—Culture Of Unfinished Thoughts and Sentences. Societies established based on how well each member finished another's thoughts or sentences are CUTS. Generated from the rule that everyone talks at once, CUTS tradition only requires that you only listen to yourself, the most important speaker.

DAMN—Don't Ask Me Now—DAMN, if I knew, I would not be looking for it or having you ask me where I left it.

Double Back—When management figures they have to hire three people to do what you did, after they fired you, then asks you to return for double your salary, you have been DOUBLE BACKED.

DBA—Disliked By All— Doing business as someone who is DBA.

DOE—Denial Of Everything. How John became DOE.

DOMO—Defer Others My Opinion. "Don't ask me; you decide what my opinion is; I am the DOMO."

DOMOCAN—Do More Than I Can. Possible virtually, or with a generous gift of fiction.

DOOMER—Director Of Obsolete Misinformation.

DOT—Designated One Thinker. The DOT is the only one allowed to think.

Doubage—Double Aged. What the organization wants to hire someone who is double their age in experience. The more it is found that this person does not exist—e.g. 30 years old with 60 years of experience—the more effort is put into finding them.

DWIP—Don't Want It Price. Price someone is willing to pay for something they don't want is the DWIP.

Diffeaser—One who is in charge of making things more difficult because it is easier than making them easier.

E2—Effortless Effort. The E2 Syndrome is demonstrated by those who can perform arduous tasks and display great talent with grace with no sign of effort.

EAT—Excitement At all Times. Eating. To compensate for all the job does not give in excitement. EAT.

EATS— Enough Aggravation To Succeed. The amount of one's success must be commensurate with the level of aggravation which has eaten away at them.

E.G.—Emotionally Gifted. One capable of overseeing a crisis without making the crisis bigger or making another one from it.

Enerkind—Just enough energy to be kind.

EST—Enemy Same Team. Your real work begins, or is ESTablished, when you realize those you are working with are working against you—that they want you to be defeated more than the people you thought both of you were competing against.

ETC.—Everyone Takes Credit. Etc. Etc.

ET—Equal Time. The total number of times you have awakened before the alarm sounds equals the total number of times you have slept through the alarm is called ET.

EUBominate—Exceeding Unlimited Budget. Someone hired with an unlimited budget, but finds a way to exceed it, eubominates.

Excuson—When the excuse for not doing is better than the reason for doing it.

Exmath—The addition of dollars to the salary of top executives, increased by the amount of salary reduced by employees at lower levels.

Eximp—Exceeding the Impossible. The constant motivating force that keeps all in an agitated state is Eximption. We might not be able to accomplish the possible, but the impossible is even more improbable.

FFF—Fiction Finding Figures; Figures Finding Fiction. Your choice, either way, merge and marry all of the Fs.

FABulous—Fired As Blessing. When you cannot get yourself to leave, the job horrible, the people worse, being fired is FABulous. You could thank them for releasing you, but they do not deserve to know the favor they did for you.

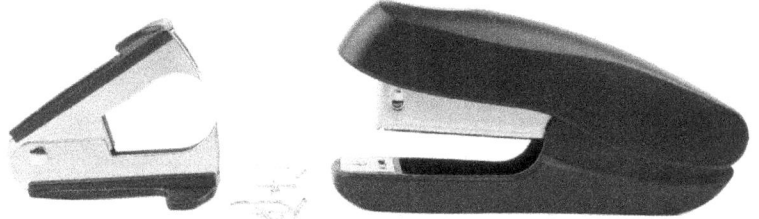

FAIR—Foregone Assumption I am Right. The most FAIR way is the one subordinates embrace as FAIR.

FEH—Fundamentally Expendable Husband.

FEW—Future Ex Wife.

FEMININE—Fire Every Male Immediately No Interruptions No Exceptions.

FILO—First In Laugh Out. The first person who could give you a bad time each day will not because through the FILO system you have been waiting for them and will laugh them right out of causing any aggravation, or difficulty.

FIT—Forever Is Tomorrow. When you have been told that you will have a job with the organization forever, it is time to upgrade your resume and start looking elsewhere for work.

FIXER—Found Inept eXpert Equal Rates. The person you called to fix it is an expert who cannot fix it. You could have paid yourself for not knowing how to fix it.

FRUTH—Someone FiRed for telling the trUTH. A FRUTH knows by experience that the truth is the best way of setting oneself free.

FLAP—FLagrant Abusive Power, without a way to stop it.

FLOP—Failed Loss Of Perspective—The only failure was a loss of perspective.

FLOUNT—FLow Of UNinterrupted Time. The FLOUNT is the amount of time people go without an interruption. FLOUNT time accumulates, and people are paid according to how well they do with how many interruptions. The FLOUNT Factor.

FOFO—Focus On Final Outcome. FOFO pawing is putting your foot and hand prints on the bodies of those you must walk on to the top of where you are going.

FOMO—Failing On My Own. Thank you for your offer to help me fail, but I prefer being on my own, I can do it alone, for I can do my own FOMOing.

FOSTER—Fast Or Slow The Exact Results. No matter how fast or slow you do your work, you will have the same results.

FOUL—For Outrage Unfair Linkage. The complaint for being blamed for someone else's mistakes.

FUG—Falsely UpGraded. When someone has been upgraded, with more money or a higher position undeservedly, they are said to have been FUGGED Up.

Funphobia—The fear of not having enough fun at work.

Fungo—The fun of any game is gone when more pressure is applied to playing it than the work one left to play it. Another name for golf is Fungo.

GACAS—Goes Around Comes Around Space. With all that is attributed to what Goes Around Comes Around, what happens to that which does not come after it has gone. Where is that space, where is all of that stored? And who is supposed to deal with it?

GAFRAN—Goals Are Forever, Results Are Now. Goals are stated and most never met, you won't be here to reach them; results are for now, as soon as you are hired the next time you are seen, what have you done, and why don't we have the results we just discussed.

GAFTing—Getting Away From Thieves. GAFTing from those at the top, and bottom and those who do it who are in between the top and bottom.

GAME—Go Away Money Earned. Money earned by leaving, or being let go. In effect, GAME is not-working money.

GAME—Got Another Meeting Everyone. The game is to keep moving, with as many people as you can get to believe that you are in the next GAME in town.

GATOSE—Go Ahead Try Offending Someone Else. The energy used to tell someone to find someone else to offend.

GEL—Good Effective Lies. The energy that keeps everyone GELing and going forward positively.

GRASP—Gross Rationalized Annual Stolen Products. The amount of stolen goods rationalized by those who have stolen, as being owed to them. Also, Gross Revenue Annual Stolen Percentage.

GIP—Giver of Infinite Patience. Too many GIPPERS, too much work undone.

GLINC—Good Looking, INCompetent, hire them.

GLEE—Greatness Less Energy Exerted. Expend less energy to gather greater results.

GM—Good Micromanager. The great obtrusive oxymoron.

GOAL—Gym Office As Lifestyle. The ultimate goal for a working environment is to have an office as a gym, and calculating exercise as the basic means for making a living.

GRIP—Gossip Rumors Inspire Productivity. When employees get a GRIP they are more productive.

GROB—Getting Rid Of Boss/Bully. Make sure you dig a hole big enough to hold both of you when you decide to try to get rid of your boss.

GROP—Getting Rid Of Perfection. Releasing the need to be perfect and feeling better for not doing the job perfectly.

GUT—Getting Used To. Energy exerted to convert annoyance into tolerance of something or someone who is abhorrent is GUTOSE.

GUTS—Getting Used To Success. It takes GUTS.

Handill—Illness caused by the shaking of hands.

HapNot—Happiness from Not being hired. Even though you went through the process of being interviewed by several people, and though you thought you wanted the job, you are glad you were not offered the job, or, if offered, you are happy you will not be taking it.

HAPPY—Hobby As Profession Pays Perfectly. Seen as a hobby, the job pays perfectly.

HELP—Has Everyone Lost Perspective.

HiGo—Hired for one thing, fired for things you were never told you would be held accountable. You were supposed to know that we were going to be evaluated on other things than what we told you. Sorry, you have to leave—you are HiGone. Even though you said you were never told, you should have known.

IBM—Insulted By Machinery. Incompetency Burgeoning Multiplies.

Impotience—The Impossibility of experiencing patience.

Jop—Job hopping at the same company, moving from one position to another just before one's incompetency is evident, is JOPPING.

Jork—Those who have joy at their job are JORKs.

JIFFY—Jobs Invented For Friends Yes. "You were created in a JIFFY just to be right here."

KNOCATOO— Not One Complaint About Themselves, Only Others. K is not pronounced. To knock or complain about others constantly, never mentioning how you might be worthy of being complained about, keeps you a KNOCATOO.

KEEP—Knows Everything Exit Proof. Someone who cannot be fired because they know too much is a KEEPer.

LABOR—Looks Animated Busy Obvious Ruse. The time spent working is less than time spent looking for ways not to be working.

LAPSE—Lacking Adequate Products and Services Equally. What we lack in product efficiency we compensate for with poor service.

LAST—Long Applause for Short Talks/Speeches. LASTing.

LAY—Laughing At Yourself. "Has the time spent laughing at others ever equaled the time spent laughing at yourself?" Go ahead, LAY it out.

LIMP—Listening is IMPossible. When you have the LIMPs you can't listen anymore. LIMP, just squeezing every ounce of energy in your body to survive and not scream, "No more, please, no more."

LOGIC—Let Others Gather In Chaos. You create your own importance by withstanding a need to be part of LOGIC.

LOOT—Leaving On Own Terms. Those who leave when they want to, with more money than the company wanted to give them, deserve praise for their LOOTing.

LORE—Lying On Resume Entices. When people are hired for the fiction on their resumes, and seemingly impossible accomplishments, it is believed that future fantasy will be created to attain greater results.

LOTTO—Letting Others Talk Themselves Out. Winning is listening and kindly letting others talk themselves out.

LOVE—Lowering Of Valued Expectations.

LUCK—Life Under Cosmic Kindness Someone else's success is easy to accept as luck.

MAGIC—Misplaced Again, Gone, I am Confused. "It's MAGIC, it was just here. Where did it go? Am I lost; does it know where I am? Or did I just disappear?"

Makimp—Making the impossible happen. "There he goes again, Makimping everything."

MANDatory—Meetings And Nothing Done. Gatherings done to remind everyone who has and who does not have the power to call a meeting where nothing gets done. The more time at meetings, and the more meetings, and the more nothing gets done, MANIC sets in—Meetings And Nothing Is Completed behavior exists.

MERIT—Making Every Right Idea Theirs. Your MERIT pay increase is based on how well you make your ideas seem to be those of your supervisors.

MEMalist—Making Everyone Miserable. A MEMal maker is one who assigns someone to be a MEMalist.

MORE—Message Only Response Electronically. More and more messages makes for less and less contact.

Minimax—The minimum amount of work for the maximum amount of pay.

MMM—Managers Managing Managers. In a state of non-doers, managers observe managers who manage managers.
MONGO—Middle Of Nothing Going On. In the center of

the universe, in the middle of the company, and from your vantage point, complete MONGO—Nothing is going on.

MOSE—Married Obsessed with Someone Else. MOSERS fantasize about having what they don't have to balance what they do, and do not always maintain a dignified balance between what they would like to have and what they don't.

MUMU—Mess Up Move Up. People who have made several costly mishaps at each position, but somehow have been awarded each time with promotions.

Musold—The music one is forced to listen to while waiting on hold for someone who is talking to someone else.

Winning Words at Work

It is important to have people in one's life who give good Musold to others.

NAP—Not Always Pleasant. A nap keeps everyone from NAPing. Also, Nocturnal Afternoon Passing.

NEDO—Neatly Disorganized. NEDO.

NEOgamy—Not Enough Oxygen in the room because of all of the egos.

NET—Not Every Thing. It is said that everything that comes around goes around. The NET holds everything that does not come around full circle.

NEWS—Noise Enhanced Willfully to Shock.

NOBLE—Not Offended By Lesser's Errors. Not upset by someone else's incapacity, errors, or misbehavior. Noble of us, of course.

Nobostelli—(No Boss Tell I.) The hard pasta one keeps in his/her mouth to prevent themselves from telling the boss what they think of them, or that they are going to quit.

Nocalbacus—Not good at calling back. One who is not good at calling back, hopes that the person who called will call again, or that they will forget they called, and if they ever confront us for not calling back, we can politely tell them that we never got the message, or that we called them, and they are the ones who are Nocalbacus.

NONE—News Obviously Not Entering. NONE, because even good news can wait, bad news I don't want to hear at all.

NOSE—Need Of Suffering Endlessly. Those who need to fight every fight, without time to heal their damages, in constant battle mode are NOSErs.

NOW—No One Wrong. The greatest moment is NOW, when no one is wrong. No blame for everyone for everything is right.

NOWAY—No One Wonderful As You. No Way.

NUTS—Not Used To Success.

OBLigatory—One Big Lie. It is your obligation to have one big lie to work with; at least one untruth to live with … Don't have one? Make one up.

Octocon—A person with the ability to do at least eight activities at once. Among them—Be on the phone, send a fax, do e-mail, listen to the radio, watch television, write, read, and pet an animal.

Organot—Someone so organized that he/she cannot get things done.

Organation—When disorganization exists so long that it becomes the new order of things, it is the new organation.

OSOPtimal—One Size Of Paper is the perfect office medium.

OTOlingus—On The Other line. OTOlingus is the pulse of the world, the constant replacing of one voice with another. You can expect someone to be communicating with someone else when you contact them, therefore everyone is living in the world of OTOlingus.

Offace—Office space marked off that is the same dimensions of the jail space one will be living in when convicted of the crime they are committing in the office.

Orchastrate—Organizing Chaos by deciding the importance of each potentially chaotic situation.

PPP—Passionately Pushing Papers. Pushing papers must show your passion for work; when papers do not look right in a vertical row, change them to go horizontal, and as your passion grows, pile them up, then unpile them and start all over. If what the papers say causes you to lose some of your passion, kindly throw them away.

Percalus—PERsonal CALis US. Personal calls that loose business.

PAD—Paper Art Design. Moving and reorganizing papers on one's desk into an art collage.

PAL—Plans And Laughter. PALs decide who will do the work. The more others do, the better pals they become.

PANIST—Paying Attention Not In Style. With the purpose of communicating being the science and art of interruption and intrusion, it is imperative to become a good PANIST.

PHOBOBO—Phone Book Bored. When you are so bored that you start looking through the phone book for people you do not know to call, you are declared PHOBOBO.

Pictavert—Someone with an aversion to seeing other people's photos of themselves, their families and total strangers.

Plabos/Plabosis—The art of taking the place of, or playing the boss.

Plunk—Planning luck. Find it, buy it, make it, but the only way to have it for sure is to plan it.

PM—Prevention Maintenance—whatever can be used to keep someone from reaching over the table and hurting someone else.

POD—Planning Own Demise. Anyone who feels that all they are doing is getting them closer to begin fired is a PODer; they are inadvertently planning their own demise.

Polifits—The amount of losses due to personal politics. The cost of winning political battles but losing company profits.

POOF—Primary One Objective Fun. The cost employers must pay for not providing an atmosphere of fun is the POOF factor.

POW—Performance Outdoes Worth. When everyone is threatened by your excellent performance, someone must find a way to POWer you out.

PRAISE—Pompous Regard And Inaccurate Self-Evaluation. Those in need of PRAISE have only to go to themselves.

Profire—When firing you is done so nicely that you feel that you have been promoted, you have been Profired.

Prognoption—Progress No Option. Go forward, yes, but Prognoption is the only result we can predict.

PUFF—Productive, Unliked Finally Fired.

PUFF—Profits Used For Fighting. The PUFF factor is the total expense utilized for fighting legal battles.

Pupship—Putting Up People Ship. Tolerating—putting up—with the excesses of human behavior.

PWOP—Person WithOut Power. A person in a power position but without the capacity or willingness to use it.

RACK—Reckless Actions Choosing Keenly. Those who ramble through rows of clothing rapidly without caring about the disorder they make as they hunt for the right color and fashion are RACKless.

RAWGO—Rules As We GO. Anything and everything that is possible finds, or makes its own way, as we RAWGO.

RATTLES—Rearranging All Things To Leave Every Second. Those who are constantly rearranging their desk and office so it looks like they are ready to leave at any time have the RATTLES.

RAM—Rage Against Machinery.

Repless—Replace Less. "Don't worry, that person did nothing. We found someone to replace him. He does less."

Referior—People who report to those inferior to them.

Requit—Resisting the urge to quit.

Revunk—When revenge is unknown by the one who is receiving it.

ROW—Regardless Of Worry. Row, Row, Row your boat of worry. Whatever is going to happen is going to happen, whatever, whomever, whenever.

SAFE—Staying Away From Evaluations.

SAINT—Surviving Another Immature Negative Tantrum.

SAME—Slower And More Efficiently. You can do it slower with the same results, SAMER.

SAMERGY—Silence As Meaning. The wisdom to say nothing is more effective than anything you can say. SAMERGY people know you can't untalk anything.

SANANYMOUS—Satisfied Absolutely No Ambition. Those whose only ambition is to have no ambition when opportunity calls are sananymous.

SANE—Still And Nothing Exciting.

SANS—Stress About No Stress People stressed because there is no stress in their jobs are SANS.

SAT of SATS—Sick And Tired of being SATS. People who are tired of sitting around being tired of everything are SAT of SATS.

SCREAM—Salaries Cause Reduction of Everyone's All around Morale. Screaming at the office begins when anyone/everyone realizes that those who are paid to play sports do not turn on any channel when they are not playing to follow the work of those who are the screamers in the office.

Scriptogize—Writing an apology for someone to give to you.

SEAT—Sit Exit Any Time. The best seat is where you can leave without anyone noticing you are gone.

Shouper—Someone who shows up to do the job, but can't, and insists on being paid for showing up is a SHOUPER.

SIBily—Stuck In Bureaucracy. Sibily is the family created by the work bureaucracy. Those who believe the people at work are in any way part of their family, are Sibilfied, and feel secure in their position within the system because they are family in sibocracy.

SIMP—Supposing Impossible Happens.

SIPrage—The rage felt and somehow contained for surviving impossible people.

SIMergy—Surviving Insufferable Meetings. The capacity to endure meetings that deplete morale and deter motivation to work. SIMergists compute their income by dividing the time they attend such meetings into the amount of their salary to find their 'real' per minute income.

Simpossible—The more effort put into making things simple results in making the process and procedure impossible to function.

SEMI—Selecting Effective Mediocre Individuals. Semitizing is hiring those who will not be a threat to those in power.

SLOP—Self-Limiting Option Person. Someone who always seeks ways to limit performance and increase compensation is the SLOPPER.

SLOG—Successful Lowering Of Goals. We might not be great, but we are successful with our SLOG. If we did not have it, we would be out of business.

SMAP—Solution Makes Another Problem.

SMAT—Something Missing All the Time. Please accept the SMATTering reality that something is always missing or misplaced. We don't need it now, but where is it?

SOB—Software On Brain. The loss of thinking that is the result of an overdependence on
computers.

SOB—Spotlight On Boss.

SOB—Some One Better. No matter how good we make it, someone out there is already making it better, or will make it better. "Remember that SOB is out there, all the time, permanently, and don't forget it."

∽ Survival Guide for an Impossible World

SOFT—Stressed Out From Tranquility.

SONNET—Saying Only Necessarily Nice Endearing Things. SONNETizing is used to make all devious moves and intent seem to disappear from another's judgment of you.

SOS—Stay On Subject. A call out in the middle of communications for someone to stay on the subject, not to deviate.

SOOO—Stating Of Obvious Obviously—As in, "SOOO what; enough already, how many times do you have to repeat what is already so obvious?"

SSS—Same Size Stationery. We might not reach a paperless office, but we can have all stationery or paper.

SSS—Stress Seeking Stress. Those without stress, who cannot create it or stress about anything eventually have to ask others if they have any ideas of how they can become stressful. SSS finders are those gifted at the art of giving others subjects to stress about.

STATIC—Steady Tension And Tumult In Concert.

STOP—Stick To Obvious Points.

Subdo—Doing the work of your subordinates. Because you are involved in doing someone else's work, you cannot do your own, and soon will have a new boss, the subordinate whose job you were doing.

Supexcusation—The state of annoyance/bewilderment when supervisors have to listen to a new excuse as to why something was not done.

Staredumb—Staring at your losing lottery numbers, and waiting for them to change to the winning ones, so you don't have to go back to work.

SWAD—Sorry, Will Again Do. No matter the apology for bad behavior, SWADers cannot help themselves, they will continue to practice bad behavior.

SWAP—Solution Without A Problem. We SWAPped priorities. Before we were looking for solutions to problems. Now we have no problems, just several solutions seeking a problem to call their own.

SWAP—Sucker With a Pen; I SWAP my debt for your willingness to pay it.

SWATT—Something Wrong All The Time. Those who believe that something is wrong or must be wrong all the time are SWATTers. Even though they do not know what it is, something has to be wrong, how else can things be?

TASK—Take Advantage of System Knowingly. The work is easy, the TASK is more difficult.

Tenplan—The tentative plan of a tentative plan.

TEE—Take Everything Everywhere. TEEing off is when you move everything everywhere and wherever you go. THIGometry—That's How It Goes. The geometry that connects things as they are, not knowing or understanding why.

TIP—Take It Personally. Warning! What happens to you is personal so take it that way. TIP.

TooToo—Too qualified (overqualified) and Too prone to leave.

TOOTS—Thinking Of Others Too, Sweetheart.

TOUR—Training One's Ultimate Replacement. The time spent training someone who will replace you. Though you are told you will move onto another position within the organization when the TOURing is completed, your best odds are that you will be moved out of the company to go on tour elsewhere.

TOY—Turning On You. The complete work experience is complete when you have been set up to fail by your fellow employees. You are the winning target, the people of the system have TOYed you out.

Triork—Work has three levels: first—when you work for someone else; second—when you and that person both work together; third—when the person you worked for now works for you.

Two-Four—When you take two weeks off work for any reason and return to find that it takes four weeks or four months to catch up with the pace of the office, you got a Two-Four. To avoid this gap, take everything you need to do while you are on vacation so you won't have to wonder what would make you happy during your time away.

VIP—Very Irritating Person.

VACA VACA—A vacation that needs a vacation as an antidote from the pain of having to return to work.

WW—Working Welfare. When you are paid for being on the job and you are not working, you are part of the Working Welfare State.

WWWWWWW—What Went Wrong With Where Why and Who.

WAIT—Why Am I talking? WAIT—The great self-imposed wake-up call questioning why I need to be talking at this moment, or at all.

WAM—Walk Around Management. A WAMer wants to be noticed more than he wants to notice how much everyone is accomplishing.

WAM—Walk Away Money. What you are paid to leave right now.

WAM—Wait A Minute.

WANGO—Waiting As Nothing Goes On. The moments spent in WANGO divided by the amount of your salary determines your real worth.

WAW—Worry About Worry. WAWing is not having enough to worry about.

WELL—Write Exit Leaving Letters. The highest state of well-being at work is reached by writing exit letters at the end of each day, and leaving them for you to review the following day. When you are fired, ask for a bonus for the time you stayed after you should have left. They should at least pay for your WELL being letters.

Whif—What If.

WHO—Work Happiness Overrated. The WHO is a group of employees who cannot find happiness at work, don't look for it there, and don't want to even make the adjustments of perspective to accept it as possible.

Winning Words at Work

WILL—Waiting In Lines Lovingly. WILLpower includes the power to withstand long lines of waiting for anything, and the decency not to offend anyone while your wait continues to continue.

WIMP—Waiting for the Impossible to Happen.

WISE—Who Isn't Stealing Enough? The question for the wise.

WISE—Whichever/Whatever/Whoever IS Easiest.

WIT—Whoever Isn't There, created and discussed by those who are.

WOH!!!—World On Hold. The only way to stop the movement of all planets and stars is for everyone in the world to be on hold for someone else at the same time.

WOD—Watching Others Do. WODing is watching others do all the work and not complaining that you are not doing it.

WOOPS—Worked Out Of Position Sorry. You worked so well, so long, and now because there is nothing else no one wants to do, you are expendable— WOOPS. Sorry — SWOOPS.

Wormore—Worry More. "The more you tell me not to worry more, the more I WORMORE."

WOTTO—Watching Others Talk To Others not in the room.

63

Survival Guide for an Impossible World

WOWO—Watching Others Watch Others. When you only watch those who are watching others, you are WOWOing.

YAB—You Are the Best. YABing yourself is reminding yourself and those who will listen that you are the best.

YADA—Yes And Do As. Tell them what they want to hear, and YADA, YADA, YADA.

YAG—You Aren't Going. No matter how well you ask, even beg, YAG, and YAG...

YAWP—Yelling At Wrong Person.

YIMP—You are Impossible.

YIP—Your Inappropriate Presence. YIPPies always say or do inappropriate things. "Yep, just another YIPpie."

YOLT—Years Of Life Taken. YOLTage is the total time and wearing of life lost on a job that is taking your life away.

YOMO—Your Office My Office. Those who bring some or all of their office equipment and apparatus to someone else's office to begin conducting their office needs are YOMOing. Also, MOYO—My Office Your Office.

HOW TO **SURVIVE** WHILE **WAITING** FOR **ANYTHING** OR **ANYBODY**

IN THE BEGINNING

In the beginning there was light and the people who did not see it were waiting for it. They became the first people ever to wait.

And waiting became such a natural element of life that the process has been passed from one generation to another, without hope or desire to diminish it until now.

"What are we doing here?" has been answered with "We're Waiting."

The answer is why wait? Now, no more victims in the waiting game.

THE FIRST WAITING TIMES

Our very first wait is the time we spend in the womb waiting to come out. Two of the longest waits involve parents and children. One has to do with who is going to grow up first, the parent or the child; the other has to do with how long the child has to wait for parents to stop telling him what to do.

WAITING QUESTIONS

What about answers to these waiting questions:

How long do you really have to wait for the cows to come home?

If you are not in a hurry, are you really waiting?

Is it possible to die waiting?

Who has waited the longest for another person to change his or her mind?

How many people have changed their college major while waiting in registration lines?

Who first declared, I don't wait for time; time waits for me?

THE WAITING PERSONALITY

There is a waiting personality: a person who likes to wait, who considers it a desirable necessity of life. The waiting person feels if there is a line he should be a part of it. He looks forward to rush hour traffic so he can share the waiting experience with millions of strangers. When cars line up to pay their toll on a turnpike, he will get in the longest line.

He never feels victimized by any element of life that makes him wait, nor does he feel swallowed up by the time given to waiting. He feels blessed to believe that being in another line is no problem.

WAITING CONCEPTS TO CONSIDER

If you were not supposed to be waiting, you would not be doing so.

Those who hate to wait are those who hate to make others wait. But sometimes their efforts to curtail waiting only have the opposite effect, more waiting for everyone.

How to Survive While Waiting for Anything or Anybody

TIPS IN A WAITING WORLD

There are some basic cures for survival in various waiting situations.

    One . . . Let others get in front of you in a line. Their surprise and appreciation will make you smile, even laugh. If you need to feel good all day, stay in that line and let everyone else go before you. Do this long enough and you can become a full-time giver of space and time to others. Are there any causes more philanthropic?

    Two . . . Use the line to help you relax. All frustrations about other things in your life can be transferred to your being stuck in the waiting position.

    Three . . . Always try to make sure someone is behind you in any line because that will give you the feeling of not having to wait the longest.

    Four . . . Tell everyone that you hold the record for waiting in the longest line. If someone says they have waited longer than you, create a better story.

    Five . . . Have someone hold your place in line while you are busy looking for another line and someone else to hold your place there.

    Six . . . Always have someone with you to share the wait.

    Seven . . . If you cannot find a friend to go along, hire a wait-mate.

> Eight . . . Ask to be compensated for any time you have waited.
>
> Nine . . . Make waiting an art form.
>
> Ten . . . What is good about waiting is that you can do it whenever and wherever you want.

LOVE DOES NOT WAIT

To those waiting and hoping someone will fly across a crowded room with instant love, stay out of crowded rooms. If you have to wait forever, you were always in the wrong place.

WAITING FOR SOMEONE TO SHOW UP

While you are waiting for people to arrive, you have these reasons to consider for their not being there as planned:

> One . . . They forgot. Think of how much you really have to be with them right now. Could it be a blessing that they did not show?
>
> Two . . . You are waiting at the wrong place, at the wrong time, and on the wrong day.
>
> Three . . . They had no intention of coming.

How to Survive While Waiting for Anything or Anybody

Four . . . They were there already and left.

Five . . . Be forgiving, and enjoy not having to do anything but wait.

Six . . . Start thinking of the excuses you are going to give those who have to wait for you.

GOVERNMENT'S SUPPORT OF WAITING: TAXES AND THE BUREAU OF WAITS

Because waiting plays such an important part of our lives the government could use it in considering our taxes. People will keep records of the time they have had to wait and of the time when they expected to wait but did not. The difference between these two figures will be computed with a per hour economic value given.

Year's reasonable waiting time .... 10,560 hours
Year's expected but unwaiting time .... - 250 hours

TOTAL   10,310 hours
At a rate of $10.00 per hour, this equals a $103,100 deduction.

THE CAR: THE GREAT MOVING WAIT

What has the auto industry given us to tolerate the driving waits we have to endure?

A car could be equipped to save us from having to shave or dry our hair at home. Millions of hours are spent sitting every day.

How about a cycling unit attached to each seat so that waiting time can be pedaled away, even converted into horsepower?

SPORTS AS A NON-WAITING GAME

Sports offers everyone a great time for waiting. The time between pitches, the time in the football huddle, the time it takes a hockey or soccer team to score, affords sports fans ample opportunity to wait.

How to Survive While Waiting for Anything or Anybody

The real winner of any game is not the player or team with the most points, but the fan who waits the least. The successful non-waiting sports fan knows how to save time and react to non-activity.

"Take me out to the ball game, but make sure I am the hero of the non-waiting game," is the theme of the wait-free spectator. No matter the sport, the non-waiter has his own game plan. He avoids the stadium food lines by eating the usual game meal at home.

GUIDELINES FOR LEAVING SPORTS EVENTS:

Baseball: The seventh inning stretch is the time to go. No matter how exciting the game is or how close the score, it isn't worth moving slowly through the waiting lines at the end of the game.

Basketball: Halfway through the fourth quarter is the time to leave, because you can listen to the last two minutes of the game on the radio.

Football: The no-wait spectator stays for a half hour after the game is over. This fan leaves with dignity, and is not a part of the mass exodus.

<u>The Waiting Players:</u> The million dollar player who plays only one percent of the entire playing time throughout the season gets paid $10,000 for playing, and $990,000 for waiting. Isn't he really the winner of the sports waiting life?

WAIT WATCHERS

Wait watchers are those who love to watch others wait. They get extreme pleasure from going by a long line of waiting people, and knowing that they are not among them. They count the people who are waiting, and deduct that number from their daily allotment of wait watching people.

TELEVISION: A TWO SET WATCHER

There are two types of television waiters: Those who wait for the commercials to come on and those who wait for the program to return.

Manufacturers of television sets can accommodate both waiting viewers with a double screen which shows commercials and programs at the same time.

How to Survive While Waiting for Anything or Anybody

THE WAITOMETER

This instrument, worn as a watch, will gauge the proper amount of time you should wait in any particular situation. When you wait beyond that time, bells will ring, and you will be required to leave.

THE LANGUAGE OF SPOKEN WAITING

How long is 'waiting' in speech? The word *wait* signifies vagueness and ambiguity. The great question arises, just how long is what a wait is?

"Wait a minute!" Is it ever a minute? Usually less. And when more, much more.

"Wait awhile" is good at vague making.

"I will not wait" strong and definite.

"I will not wait any longer than I have to" semi-submissive.

"I will wait for a while" tolerant.

"I can't wait to tell you" excitement which means there is nothing but waiting until the person is told. The answer is just as unwaitable, "I can't wait to hear."

꿍 Survival Guide for an Impossible World

When someone is 'running late' don't you want to know how fast they are running and if you start running too, will the wait take as long?

GUIDE TO WAITING LITERATURE

Waiting in the Wings . . . Noel Coward
Waiting in Style . . . Alyson Fendel
The Waiting Game . . . Eve Bunting
The Waiting World . . . Archie Matson
The Waiting Sands . . . Susan Howatch
The Waiting Room . . . John Bowen
Waiting for Shiela . . . John Braine
Waiting for the Barbarians . . . J.M. Coetzee
Waiting for the End . . . Leslie Fiedler
Waiting for Cordelia . . . Herbert Gold
Waiting for Godot . . . Samuel Beckett
Waiting for Lefty . . . Clifford Odets
Waiting for the King of Spain . . . Diane Wakoski
Waiting for the Parade . . . John Murrell
Waiting for Willa . . . Dorothy Eden

SURVEY OF WRITING QUOTES

"I have driven through the Southwest many times, and even more often have flown over it—a great and mysterious wasteland, a sun-punished place. It is a mystery, something concealed and waiting...."
—from *Travels with Charley* by John Steinbeck

How to Survive While Waiting for Anything or Anybody

"Everyman can perform; everyman can reach his goal, if he can think, wait, and fast."
—from *Siddhartha* by Herman Hesse

"And I am waiting for a rebirth of wonder ... and I am waiting for life to begin and I am waiting for the storms of life to be over...."
—from *A Coney Island of the Mind*
by Lawrence Ferlinghetti

"I don't love you at all. Wait for someone who does."
—from *The Rich Boy* by F. Scott Fitzgerald

"And Sam began to wait as if waiting were an event of great activity."
—from *Laughing Sam* by William Saroyan

"It was the severe depression brought on by the eight days imprisoned in traction—and by the thought of waiting it out as is—that sent him running to the psycho analyst."
—from *The Anatomy Lesson* by Philip Roth.

In the movie *Ronin*, someone tells Robert De Niro, "We have to do something." De Niro answers, "We are. We're going to wait."

◈ Survival Guide for an Impossible World

Laugh it off

Laugh it Off

The Guide gives you diets that you can laugh at while you lose weight safely. Are you afraid of small portions, want romance diets to mend broken hearts, or to lose weight while you are driving? How about a sport-watching diet, or a sexless generation of weight loss?

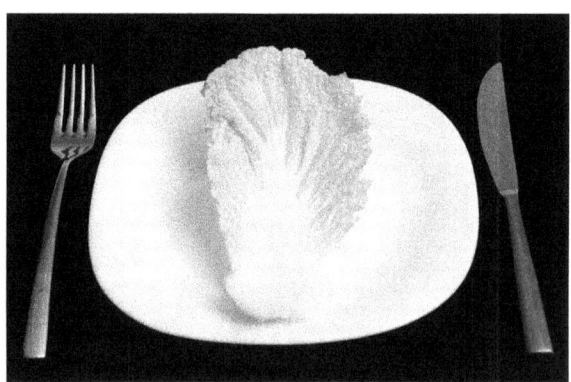

Afraid to go on vacations because of how much you will eat? Have you dealt with the connection between who you are now and who you will be in your next life?

LAUGHING IT OFF REQUIRES:

Returning to infant eating patterns as a way to weight loss.

Tax deductions for losing and maintaining a certain weight.

A sexless generation's guide to weight loss.

Romance diets which mend broken hearts.

Losing weight in any vehicle.

The space program's impact on weight reduction.

Sleep dieting.

Designer clothes and foods.

Sexist diet talk.

Losing weight without ever having to go on a diet.

Diets for sports fans.

The restaurant's role in weight loss.

"I don't ever diet," said Susan, "But if I ever had to, I'd like to have fun doing it. People have fun eating it all, why shouldn't they have fun taking it off."

Susan, this section is for you and those who would like to laugh it off. You should gain 40 pounds so that you can see how much you can laugh while taking it off.

NEW LIFE DIET

Knowing who you are going to be in your next life could influence how diet-conscious you have to be in this one.

Once you find that you will return with a faster metabolism (allowing you to burn calories much faster than you do now) you can eat what you want!

Instead of reducing your intake now, you will want to begin practicing for the next time around, when you can eat everything all the time.

PANAREXIA

Panarexia makes it possible for you to move to another place so that you do not have to go on any type of diet. Concern with equalizing weight distribution throughout the world requires people placing themselves properly to help promote a balanced movement of all elements in space.

The International Society for Interspacial Weight Alignment will identify your proper place on earth. This human relocation process is imperative in keeping the earth moving constantly through space.

ROMANCE DIET

Breaking up is not hard to do, especially if you can lose weight.

The romantic diet for break-up lovers is not to eat until you have written the story of your love affair. If that does not take very long, and you find yourself having to eat while telling the truth to your Very Personal Computer, force yourself to continue not eating until editors of local teenage magazines print your love lost results in a story that has been written and translated into current teenageze.

Make a rule for all of your romance: "I'll break up to break down my body fat."

WATERING HOLE DIET

Time to get back to where watering holes are just what they are said to be, watering holes.

Water, yes, water, water . . .

For sobriety as well as fat reduction.

How come no one has thought of water being the only thing being served at a watering hole?

Water on the rocks . . .

Water cocktails, without even a touch of diet soda, no twist, no olive, no salted rim.

Water parties, where everyone brings their own.

Waterholics Anonymous is a support group for those who are afraid to tell anyone that all they want to drink is water.

THE BORN-AGAIN DIET

The time of your birth or conception may be responsible for your overweight condition.

To be born again under another galaxy of astrological stars, arrange to have your birthday changed. Do it officially at your local hall of records.

After establishing the new date, calculate how much you have lost from the time of the date change to the new birthday. If you haven't lost enough, change the date again, and keep changing it until you have found the right date for you.

Side effects: The seeking of this new date could cause a reverse weight effect. If every day becomes your next birthday, soon you will be the only one attending your parties, without anyone else to share the cake.

THE NOT-SO-NEXT-GENERATION DIET

There can never be enough support groups to keep some people away from violating the world's need for cosmic caloric sanity. To eliminate this network against excessive human weight, everyone must weight the same. To reach this utopia there first must be a very fat generation, followed by a not-so-skinny generation, followed by a not-so-not-so fat generation, to be followed by a not-so-not-so skinny generation, etc., and etc., and etc.

TRAVEL WEIGHT CONTROL

The travel industry can make its fares encourage weight control. All travelers should be charged for how many pounds they bring on board. Instead of classes based on the ability to pay, differences in ticket prices will be based on human weight.

Here is the bill of extra fare for those flying one way from Los Angeles to New York using the new Human Pounds Method

Price	Weight
100 dollars	150 pounds and less
150 dollars	151 to 200 pounds
200 dollars	201 to 250 pounds
250 dollars	251 to 300 pounds
300 dollars	301 pounds to infinity

Other forms of transportation can use similar types of pricing. A car dealer can base his or her price on the weight of the principal driver of the car, charging more to heavier customers.

Turnpike tolls could reflect weight carried in passenger cars with charges varying according to total car and passenger pounds.

WATCHERCIZERS BURN-OFF DIET

How many ounces do you think you can burn off watching others exercise? How many pounds can you lose watching others resist another pound of fattening foods?

Watchercizers think plenty. Watchercizers lose weight by watching others.

Watchercizers claim that they can lose 20 percent of all the calories they have gained by observing 30 minutes of someone else's workouts or dietary practices. Some even found they have lost weight by watching others gain pounds.

FREE TRIPS AND WEIGHT LOSS DIET

Having trouble deciding where to go on your next vacation? Afraid that any place you go means more pounds being produced on the body? Not willing to pay for the expense of getting there only to come home to pay for weight reduction classes?

No problem; Don't make the trip.

Stay home, buy maps of the places you wanted to go and put them on your walls.

Find out what foods are served in the places you wanted to go and eat them in portions equal to the amounts of food served on an airplane.

With the money you are saving, and the weight you are losing you can buy the outfit you couldn't have afforded or fit into had you gone.

To completely function on real travel time, contact your favorite airlines to find out when they serve passengers so that you can eat at the same time as the people who are going to the places pictured on your wall.

SEATED BY WEIGHT

What better place to influence people to lose weight than a restaurant. There are no-smoking sections, what about arranging people's seating according to weight, skinny sections, chubby sections, etc.

What you weigh determines where you will eat. Each restaurant is free to create its own seating standards. Customers will be weighed before they are seated and served.

REGULATION FOR ALL-YOU-CAN-EAT RESTAURANTS

The All You Can Eat industry can and should be regulated by the Food and Drug Administration for excessive indulgences.

1. Limit the number of times anyone can eat at these restaurants in a day, week, month, and year.

2. Limit the days of the week that these restaurants can offer All You Can Eat meals.

3. Limit the amount of food eaten by one person at one meal.

4. These restaurants should have the right to tell over-indulging patrons, "Sorry, that's enough," and allow customers a discount based on what they didn't eat, but would have liked to.

STRANGER'S SURPRISE DIET

The most exciting and least self-conscious diet of all is the Stranger's Surprise. Though it does not guarantee weight loss, it allows you not to have to think about what you are going to eat next.

All you have to know before going to a restaurant is which person sitting at what table will be the stranger whose order you will copy.

The Repeat-Seat Surprise Diet is a slight variation. It requires you to order the exact meal as the person who ate at your table, in your exact seat, before you arrived.

THE PETTING DIET

People have reduced their blood pressure by caring for pets. Now they can avoid eating that second and third dessert by petting an animal.

Restaurants that care about your weight will give you the option of petting an animal. A pettable animal will arrive with the dessert tray.

Hopefully the dieter will opt for the petting instead of the eating.

People with cat or dog allergies can pet a friend and train themselves to choose petting instead of desserting.

DIET ACCESSORIES

These are products to keep you in line; devices that will keep you honest to any of the diets you are trying to follow.

One: A horn that sounds whenever you have exceeded your limit.

Two: A fork that folds when you are about to go over your prescribed amount of calories.

Three: A plate that moves whenever you or someone else begins to serve you an excessive portion.

INFANT MIMICRY DIET

Think small, very small, to the time when you were fed by someone else. Now you are ready to change one of the most significant elements in weight loss: your body image.

All you need for Infant Mimicry is another person who wants to redesign their shape and mental form.

By feeding each other you will return to your earliest eating age, and soon you will want only children's portions for meals.

This program can continue until you reach the point of being tired of picking up the fork and spoon you have dropped or thrown on the floor.

COUNTER'S DIET

Count the number of lima beans on your plate, the number of lentils in your soup.

Count the number of bubbles in your carbonated drink, and the number of calories in everyone else's drink.

Count the number of calories on everyone else's plate.

Count the calories on everyone else's plate out loud and count how long you are welcome at the table.

MORSEL APPREHENSION

Afraid to have just a small bite of anything?

Learn to eat less by dividing your overhanging plateful so that you can begin eating less and less and enjoying yourself more and more   Here's how:

Sit down to a meal with two or three extra plates. Take a bite of food.

The next fork or spoonful put on another plate. The next spoon or forkful put on the next plate. The next on the next plate.

Continue until you are finished eating.

Wrap the food on the other plates for your next meal. Repeat this process at the next meal, and the next meal until you only want to take small bites and will demand small portions.

RECIPE FOR THE COOKIE HUGGING DIET

Take a friend to a cookie counter.

Hug your friend every time you decide not to eat another cookie.

More hugs and less cookies, thank you.

The more you hug your friend in the cookie store or by the cookie jar at home the less time you will have to eat or bake cookies. Do not try to hug your friend while trying to bake. Instead of baking, hug.

If you have a friend who refuses to hug without eating cookies, find another cookie counter.

FEDERAL WEIGHT LOTTERY

The government can make money from Weight Loss, too. A lottery!!!

1. You buy a weight lottery card which has your lucky ideal weight number.

2. If you diet to your weight number within a three-month period and maintain your weight for another three-months, you win.

3. All monies made by the government from the lottery will be given to public education on proper nutrition and how not to have to live a life of constant dieting.

4. If you do not diet and maintain the weight loss, you will have to buy more lottery cards.

5. Note: The USA is the first country to have a secretary of Human Weights and Measures.

THE IRS HEAVY TAX

The government can enter the weight loss industry for the benefit of everyone.

An automatically audited weight control system will reward those who maintain a healthy weight, paid for by those who don't. Those who do not lose an expected amount and those who do not maintain the ideal weight will pay a fee/penalty per pound.

This Heavy Tax is administered to encourage dieting and general personal health.

Now, finally, the government will have sanctioned some people actually living off the fat of the land.

LOSER'S CLOSET

No more alterations.

The clothes you have do not have to be thrown away; they can be exchanged at Loser's Closet where the people who have been on diets meet to give their recently needed to be discarded clothes away.

At the exchange you bring in your clothes and exchange them with others.

You will feel better every time you come in with your clothes and find someone there who is glad to take them.

SPORTS FAN'S DIET

Bet the games, and can't stand how little you control the final score? Eat yourself up trying to cover the point spread? The Sports Fan's Diet, usually referred to as the Sports Bettor's Diet, can rid you of the need to self-destruct trying to get your team to win for you by eating.

Here's the way to victory over eating while you wait to the end of any contest.

ONE: Turn off the television or radio during time-outs.

TWO: Chew on look-alike sports foods such as hot dogs and pretzels during the game. Rubberized productions of these foods can be chewed to give you the feel of eating while not having the add-on results gained through digestion.

THREE: Wear a helmet complete with mouthpiece that helps you restrain yourself from eating. When times get desperate you can chew out frustration by biting the mouthpiece.

FOUR: To help you resist overindulging while watching an event, an instant replay of your eating will be fed into a computer that calculates your caloric score. If you exceed the safe amount, the television or radio will automatically turn off. This computer control system will monitor your moves. An alarm will automatically be sounded throughout the neighborhood if you go next door to your neighbor to watch the rest of the game.

BEING SINGLE IS A DANGEROUS SPORT.

Those who do not believe it are not out there amidst the risks and drawbacks of single life. They are not dealing with the extreme conditions of alternative single love lands.

Subjects discussed: Being single as a source of elusive chemistry, single as a lonely art form, sites for manifesting single fictions, single as the species of the first conclusion, and bruised songs of single love.

Being Single is a Dangerous Sport is the story of uninhibited self-indulgence that pervades the lives of those living in the various disunited states of single consciousness.

Their points of view are stated here so that all can recognize that with all the fun they went after, it wasn't so much fun after all.

Being Single is a Dangerous Sport

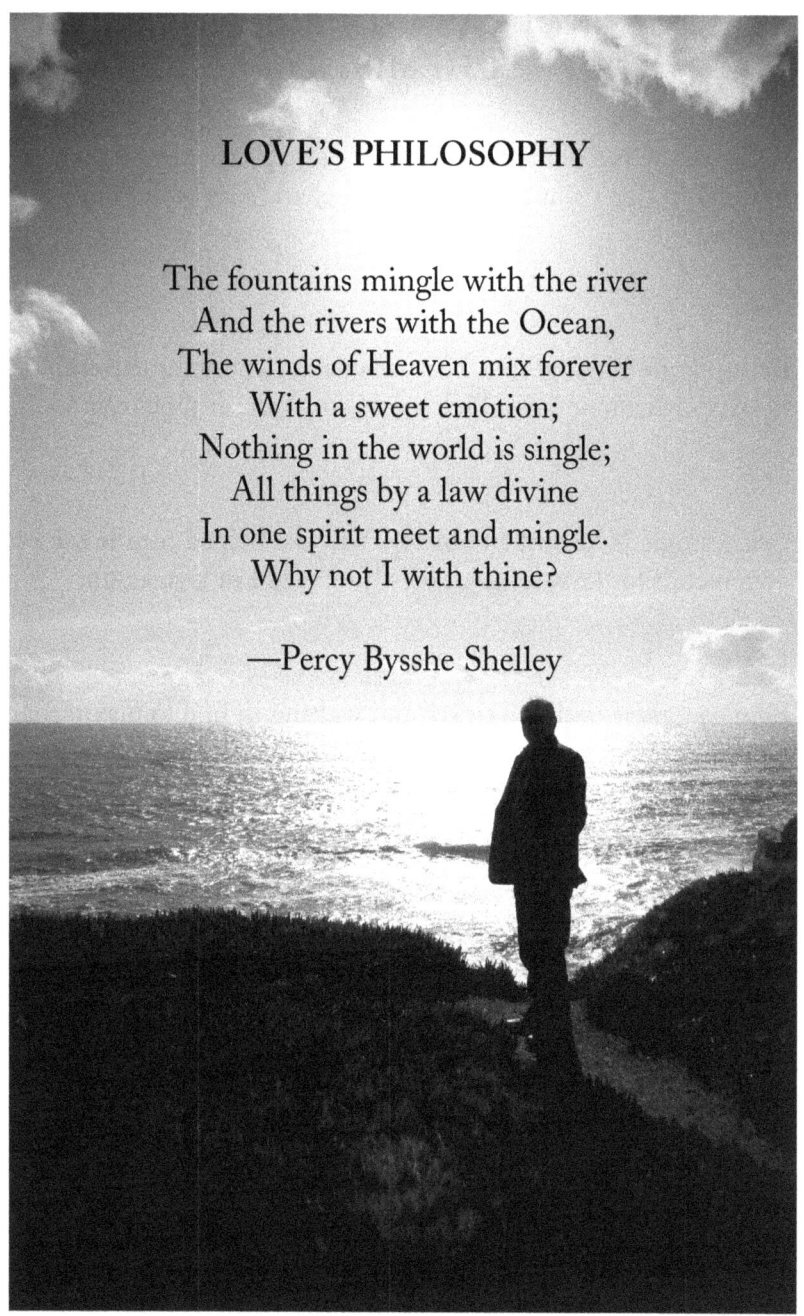

LOVE'S PHILOSOPHY

The fountains mingle with the river
And the rivers with the Ocean,
The winds of Heaven mix forever
With a sweet emotion;
Nothing in the world is single;
All things by a law divine
In one spirit meet and mingle.
Why not I with thine?

—Percy Bysshe Shelley

BEING SINGLE AS A SOURCE OF ELUSIVE CHEMISTRY

Being single is a dangerous sport because you're always on the move. You don't want to catch anyone, and you better not get caught.

Being single is dangerous because you are always at the emotional amusement park. Pick a ride, any ride. It'll be over soon.

Being single is instant chemistry. You just helped him break his own record for how long it takes him to fall in love again.

Being single is taking a ticket and waiting in line to play romantic ping-pong.

Beware! Danger! Watch out! Confusion ahead! He does not want a commitment of long-range consequence, but if there's no future in it for him, then he's not interested in it at all. It's over before it began.

Being single is remaining single because you live in the hope that the next one you meet will be from out of town so you can have a short, fast, immediate intimacy with her or him and be back-on-the-streets single again.

Being single just takes a minute. You can sign your final divorce decree and turn around to sign to be married again.

Being single is dangerous because you always say yes whenever anyone says they've got just the right person for you.

Being single is a full-time sport, keeping everyone's married hands off your single body.

SINGLE AS A LONELY ART FORM

Being single is the center of ambivalence when you find someone with everything you want and all of a sudden you're not a person who wants what he wants.

Being single puts you right in the middle of the evolving unknown. The women you meet need a man in their lives, but so far don't know what for.

Being single is dangerous when you want to be born again under a new astrological sign.

Being single is a hurting heart when the girl who just said she is crazy about you and the magic you have together is more crazy about going back to her husband, and "Besides," she tells you, "you're much better off being single, anyway."

Being single and staying single are always possible when you refuse to meet anyone unless they are married, have four children, and are happy that way.

Being single is a sad case of misrepresentation when you stay home, not answering your phone so people will think you're out swinging singlely.

Being single is a secret, when you find one guy to hide behind from all the rest.

Being single is dangerous when it reaches the loneliest of all lonely conditions: all the women you know don't want anything to do with you, and those who don't even know you feel the same way.

Being single is having a no-name offense---the girl you met last night and want to see again and again forgets your name when introducing you to the guy she just met.

SINGLE SOLUTIONS TO OVERNIGHT PHENOMENA

Being single is eating breakfast with your instant family--kids you did not know were there the night before.

Being single is needing a Saturday and Sunday morning survival kit, because someone is there who shouldn't be, or no one is there at all.

SITES FOR MANIFESTED SINGLE FICTIONS

Being single is trying to make loving you forever last longer than an hour.

Being single is delusionary and dangerous when you enter a large ballroom of dancing singles and feel you belong to every woman in the room.

Being single makes it impossible to get anywhere when all the women you want to get to know at the singles dance come only for a chance to meet their girlfriends.

Being single is when you're in the hot tub of instant magic—where you can warm your troubled single spots.

BRUISED SONGS OF SINGLE LOVE

Being single is a hopeless vision because all of the good ones are already gone.

Being single is dangerous when you start counting relationships in terms of hours and days and wonder why the longest full-timer only lasted four days.

You try so hard to analyze how things are going, you've got to look up at the clock every ten minutes to take the emotional temperature of the relationship.

Being single is staying single because you can't find a ready-made, off-the-rack woman---no alterations required.

Being single is being used as transitional therapy when a divorcing wife says, "I have to have you between my husband and a good, solid relationship."

Being single is dangerous when you have to out-wrestle sons of divorced lovers who are bigger than you, and who still are not ready for anybody but Daddy coming home.

Being Single is a Dangerous Sport

Being single is listening to her talk about her list of losers and wondering how you're going to be described.

Being single is intolerably boring when every girl tells you, "I can't help it, I fall in love with every guy I meet."

Being single is only fair when you can get insurance against the wrong type of crazymaker tempting you into their emotional grasp.

Being single is dangerous when the only women who call are ex-girlfriends who want to renegotiate.

Being single means you have to do the driving. Your non-single friends want to see you, but it's always easier for you to come over.

Being single again is being able to double date with your daughter because the "new girl" in your life is one of her best friends.

Being single is a terminal affair because those who say they don't want to be single forever wait too long—and soon it's too late.

SINGLE AS THE
SPECIES OF THE FIRST CONCLUSION

Being single has its own language and defines whatever you have not as a relationship, but as a whatever-it-is-ship.

Being single is deceptive because most married people can't believe anything could be wrong with being single.

Being single is not an enviable position when all your married friends are having a happier singles life than you.

Being single is dangerous to you and the rest of society when you have just set the world's record for the most single things ever done.

GIFTS TO A FRAGILE BALANCE

Being single is a fragile solution with inconclusive evidence.

Being single is always goodbye, but not forever because you can always meet again. You may have to.

Being single is not the best way to live longer.

Being single is safe--kind of--because you can always threaten to send him back to his second or third wife.

Being single gets sticky when you break up and try to divide the communal emotional property.

Being single could be psychologically dangerous when someone wants to take you to court for a breach of emotional promise, "For all the time I wasted with you when I could have been looking for someone who really cared."

Being single so many times in so many ways, you have to take a year off to become resolutely celibate from all emotional and physical entanglements.

Being single and staying single is easier than doing anything about it.

Being single is accountably unfair when you can't deduct the monetary and emotional expenses from your income tax form for the times you tried in vain to have a good singles time.

Being single is not much fun when all the computer matchmaker services refund their finder's fee to you as the first person they could not find anyone for.

Being single is telling your therapist you're trying when you go to a singles party once every six months.

Being single cannot always be relieved by getting married, although it would give you the chance to call your single friends more dangerous than you.

Being single is over when after years of looking--wanting and not wanting to settle down--you take the hand of a stranger in a short elevator ride--and before you tell her anything, she says, "Yes, I'll marry you. I am just as single and as dangerous as you, and if we both don't decide to act now, we're doomed to dangerous singleness forever."

Being Single is a Dangerous Sport

www.ingramcontent.com/pod-product-compliance
Lightning Source LLC
Chambersburg PA
CBHW071722040426
42446CB00011B/2176